Incredible
Butterflies

By Susan Ashley

Gareth Stevens
Publishing

Please visit our website, www.garethstevens.com. For a free color catalog of all our high-quality books, call toll free 1-800-542-2595 or fax 1-877-542-2596.

Library of Congress Cataloging-in-Publication Data

Ashley, Susan.
Incredible butterflies / Susan Ashley.
    p. cm. — (The incredible world of insects)
Includes index.
ISBN 978-1-4339-4580-9 (pbk.)
ISBN 978-1-4339-4581-6
ISBN 978-1-4339-4579-3 (library binding)
1. Butterflies—Juvenile literature. I. Title.
QL544.2.A843 2012
595.78'9—dc22

                               2010035221

New edition published 2012 by
Gareth Stevens Publishing
111 East 14th Street, Suite 349
New York, NY 10003

New text and images this edition copyright © 2012 Gareth Stevens Publishing

Original edition published 2004 by Weekly Reader® Books
An imprint of Gareth Stevens Publishing
Original edition text and images copyright © 2004 Gareth Stevens Publishing

Designer: Daniel Hosek
Editors: Mary Ann Hoffman and Kristen Rajczak

Photo credits: Cover, pp. 1, 5, 9, 13, 15, 19, 21 Shutterstock.com; pp. 7, 17 © Brian Kenney;
p. 11 © William Weber/Visuals Unlimited.

Printed in the United States of America

CPSIA compliance information: Batch #CS11GS: For further information contact Gareth Stevens, New York, New York at 1-800-542-2595.

Contents

Boldface words appear in the glossary.

Changes

Butterflies are insects. All insects change as they grow. Butterflies change more than any other insect.

Egg

Butterflies lay eggs on leaves. The eggs **hatch**. A **larva** crawls out of each egg.

egg

larva

Caterpillar

The larva is a caterpillar. The caterpillar eats the leaf. As it grows, it **sheds** its skin. Then it grows new skin. It does this many times.

9

The caterpillar sticks itself to a **twig** or leaf. It hangs upside down. It sheds its skin again.

11

Pupa

The larva becomes a **pupa**. It forms a cocoon around itself. Inside, things are happening!

cocoon

The cocoon breaks open.

A butterfly comes out!

Butterfly

A butterfly has tiny **scales** on its wings. The scales give the wings color. They give the wings a **pattern**.

Butterflies fly when their bodies are warm. You can see them on hot, sunny days.

Some butterflies **hibernate**. Some fly to warm places in winter. In spring, they fly back. They **mate**. They lay eggs. The **cycle** starts again!

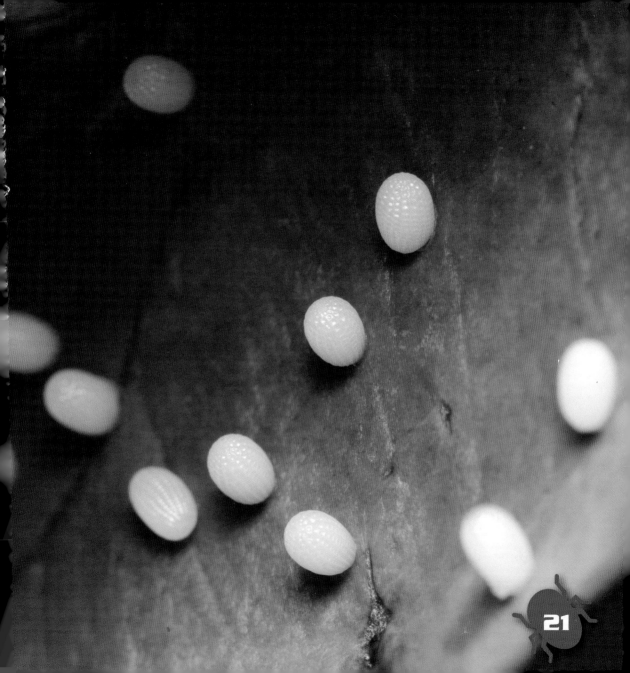

Glossary

cycle: a series of events that happen over and over

hatch: to come out of an egg

hibernate: to spend the winter resting, without eating

larva: the stage between egg and pupa

mate: to come together to make babies

pattern: colors and shapes ordered in a certain way

pupa: the stage between larva and adult

scale: one of several small, flat plates that overlap each other

shed: to get rid of

twig: a small shoot or branch

For More Information

Books

Brust, Beth Wagner. *Butterflies*. Peru, IL: Wildlife Education, 2010.

Hurtig, Jennifer. *Butterflies*. New York, NY: Weigl Publishers, 2008.

Web Sites

Butterflies at the Field Museum
www.fmnh.org/butterfly/
Discover facts about butterflies and where they live. See pictures of many different butterflies.

Butterfly Website
butterflywebsite.com
Find articles, photographs, videos, and stories about butterflies.

23

Index